TABLE OF CONTENTS

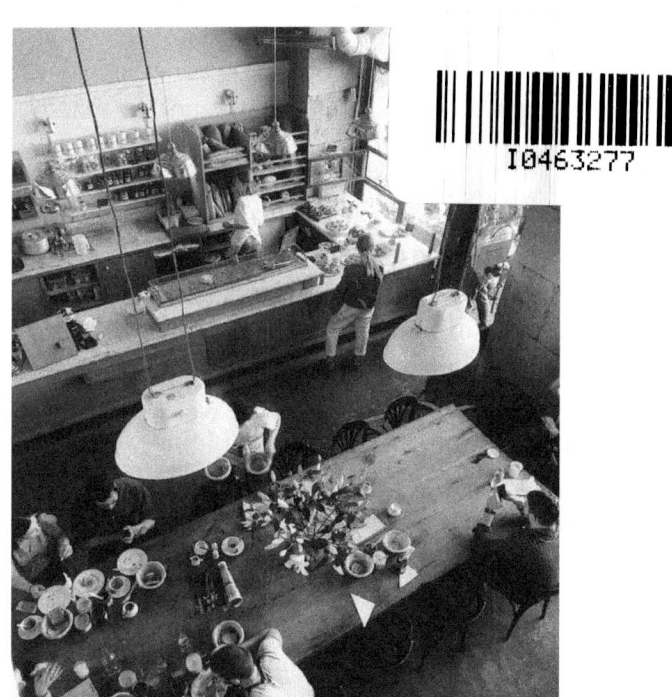

I0463277

Have you ever gone to a bar or restaurant (or own one) that has the **BEST** food, but *LOUSY* service? I have been to many of these establishments. If you have been told you have lousy service, I can help your business thrive!

The problem begins at the top with management. Managers hire employees and assume those employees know what it takes to work in a restaurant or bar. Well, that's not always the case. Every place I have worked, I heard the same thing from the newbie employees. *Why do they want it this way? Why won't they change? My way is so much better!* Well, first, if your way is so much better, why don't you own your own place?

The first thing that's **IMPERATIVE** for employees to learn is that it is *YOUR* business and things must be done the way you want them done. If your employees can't grasp this concept, then possibly you need new employees. You have put everything into this business, not the employee, and it must flourish. If you lose your business, they only lose their job. You lose everything.

My book will talk mostly about the restaurant industry because this is one of the hardest businesses to make work, one of the most difficult to keep lucrative, and to keep honest, hard-working employees.

Just remember two **VERY** important things…

NEVER, NEVER, NEVER ignore a customer; and **ALWAYS**, no matter how hard it may be, **SMILE**!!

You have no idea how a smile can change a person's entire day! These two dynamics can make or break a business and your source of income.

Chapter 1

Host or

Hostess

"The greeter needs to help make the customer forget their bad day and enjoy themselves from the moment they walk in!"

Who is the first person a guest makes eye contact with or greets? Normally, it is the host or hostess (we will refer to them as the "greeter"). Can the greeter make or break the guests visit? **YES! Most definitely!** Your greeter needs to be Happy this guest decided to come there, or at least make that guest feel they are happy to see them. There are many other restaurants they can go to, and believe me, they will. Remember, word of mouth is the best or worst advertising there is.

I will be the first person to admit that it's not always easy to be happy and upbeat at work. You may have a problem at home with a co-worker or a health problem, but the guest doesn't want to know it. They came to forget about their problems and have a good time, enjoy good food, and good service. The old saying still goes today, "Leave your problems at the door!"

When I enter a restaurant and the greeter is like "How many?" with no enthusiasm, drive, or personality, I'm not happy right off the bat. I feel like they couldn't care less if I were there or not. The greeter needs to be positive and honestly want that guest to have a great experience! A greeter should say something like, "Hello, welcome to _____, thanks for stopping in. How many tonight? Would you prefer a booth, table, or maybe a seat at the bar, or would you like to go outside on our patio (if applicable)?"

When the guests are seated say, "Your server will be ____, and he/she will be right with you." Don't just drop the menus and walk away. If the servers are busy and time allows, the greeter should offer to get them a beverage while they wait. If the guest is recognized they feel like they matter to the greeter, and then they feel like they matter to the **ENTIRE** establishment and will patiently wait. You would not believe the bearing that first "meet" can make on a person. Customers can see if it's busy or not and so long as they are acknowledged, they feel better and won't mind waiting a little.

Imagine you have an office job in customer service. All day long, for eight hours, your phone rings and everyone on the other end is dissatisfied about something. Of course, you are the one that is going to catch hell from them, even if it was another department or your supervisor's wrongdoing. No matter the situation, *YOU* answered the phone, so *YOU* are getting the rash of it! You're on the phone, trying to smooth things over with unruly and angry people who are yelling and cussing at you all day. Finally, 5:00 comes and yes, time to go home. Oh, what a catastrophic day! You don't feel like cooking or cleaning. You are completely mentally exhausted. You call your husband, wife, friend, kids, whoever, and go to _____ for dinner to relax and unwind.

Which of the two scenarios would make you feel better when you walk in the door?

1.   You walk in and you hear someone say with little or no eye contact, "How many? (Sigh) Follow me." There's no enthusiasm. It's like you don't exist. Then that person takes you to your table, plops the menus down and leaves.

Does this make you feel better yet? I don't think so. Or,

2.   You walk in and someone is standing there smiling at you and says, "Hi, welcome to _____. We're so happy you came in! Where would you be comfortable sitting this evening?" You are then taken to your table and the greeter says, "Your server will be _____, he/she will be with you soon. We're a little busier than normal right now, could I get you something to drink while you wait?"

Now, I bet, just from that initial greeting, you are starting to feel better.

A person can tell when someone has had a rough day. I know my forehead wrinkles and I look mad at the world. Some people show it in their eyes or in their body language, etc. The greeter needs to be aware of these signs and help that person forget about their bad day. Enjoying themselves from the moment they walk in the door is the goal!

Keep in mind, people will always remember their first impression of a place, so make it a great one! The greeter **MUST** be fantastic at what they do!!!

Chapter 11

Wait Staff

"I can't tell you how many times I've never gone back to a restaurant because of the service I received. On the flip side, I've gone back many times because of the service I received. What type of restaurant would you prefer?"

OMG!! How much money you make depends totally on **YOU**!!! I can't emphasize this enough! Servers repeatedly said, "Why did that table stiff me? I took their order, brought their food and went back to give them the check. I always seem to get the worst tippers!"

Hello? Did you ever think it might be **YOU**? Did they need something during their meal that they didn't get because you didn't check on them? Oh, you didn't go back and check on them? Well, that's why you got stiffed. It has nothing to do with the establishment or the customer. It had **EVERYTHING** to do with **YOU** and **YOUR** attitude!!!!

No one is to blame for you not making money as a server except you. Plain and simple! I'm not saying to go back so many times that you become a pest, but particularly if you have a food runner, make sure you are at the table when the food is delivered in case something was forgotten. It's not the runner's job to assure everything is there. It's *YOURS*!!!! Make sure they have everything they need, then give them a few minutes and check back to see if everything tastes good. Ask if they need more to drink.

A bad wait staff can break a restaurant and if the restaurant has complaints on the wait staff, they should weed them out accordingly. I can't tell you how many times I've never gone back to a restaurant because of the service I received. On the flip side, I've gone back many times because of the service I received.

I worked at this restaurant and there was one problem server. The boss chose to get rid of everyone but her because she felt sorry for her. Well, business declined, and the owner learned the hard way. So, if there's an issue with one server, get rid of <u>THAT</u> server, not everyone else. There is no place for "feelings" when it comes to your business. While this is sometimes one of the hardest things for employers to deal with, they must look out for their business first!

All servers must walk a fine line in order to be successful. If you have repeat customers, you will soon learn the customers you can harass and the ones you can't. Once you figure out the ones you can play around with **DO** it! They will love it and keep frequenting the establishment. They will probably ask for YOU each time! People want to laugh and have fun and if you can give that to them, you can be very successful!!!

I want my server to be friendly and harass me a little because I'm going to harass them, just to see if they can take it. I don't mean it as being rude. I mean playful. Ask them their name and tell them yours. A little later ask them what your name is and see if they remember. A good server will come back before you have the chance to ask them and ask, "How's it going Donna? Is everything all right? Do you need anything right now?" If they call you by your name, you know they care about their job and about you and your experience. They will reap the rewards in the tip. I like to call on the phone when I know the place well. It breaks up the monotony and everyone has a good laugh.

I'll say something like, "Hello, Sarah, table three would like more water please." She just turns and looks at me and bursts out laughing. Then she tells all the other servers. They all love it. It keeps them going a little longer and guess what? They're all smiling!!!

PLEASE PLEASE PLEASE DO <u>NOT</u> refer to your customers as honey, baby, sweetie or sugar pie unless that customer is your honey, baby, sweetie or sugar pie. This is one of the most aggravating things you can say as a server. I can't think of anything that upsets me more, specifically when it's a nineteen or twenty-year-old calling me honey! OMG! Please don't do it!

Ladies, have you ever worked with male servers who make twice as much money as you even when they don't give as good service? Or here's a good one. A male server has a table and he's not busy, but the table stops you to ask for more water, bread, etc., because he is nowhere around? Let me tell you why. People feel the male server has a family to support and needs the money more than a female server. **I KNOW**!! So, biased!!!! People are under the assumption, even today, that the male is the main source of income in the family and should be the bread winner. This is predominantly true with an older clientele.

I once worked with a guy whose name was Jerome. There weren't many male servers then. We had the same number of tables throughout the night, but at the end of our shift he made one-third more money than I did. Some of his customers left him a five-dollar tip when those same customers, on other nights, only left me three dollars. I thought Jerome may have been related to them or something, but he said no. Also, I knew these customers very well. The next time they came in, I asked them if I gave them bad service or if they had a problem with me.

They said no and that they gave him five dollars and me three because he was a man and a man must support his family. I laughed at this response because Jerome was single, and I was a single mother. WHAT A JOKE!!! I never told the customer that, but OMG what nerve and misconceptions people have. There is nothing you can do about the delusions people have about men and women workers. Don't let it get to you. Shake it off and do the best possible job you can!

NEVER NEVER NEVER touch your hair, your eyes or pick your teeth while waiting on customers or where customers can see you! I worked with a server, and she would be at a table taking an order with her finger in her mouth, picking her teeth and asking what she could get them! OMG!! GROSS!

If I were that customer, I would have walked right out of that place. I tried to say something to her, but she didn't believe me. We all do things unconsciously, but you must pay attention to what you are always doing with your hands when you are a server because YOUR hands will be delivering the food.

My husband and I were at a local restaurant that we frequent. I saw a waitress in the area where you pick up food taking her pony tail out and redoing it right there by all the food. There was no sink for her to wash her hands. When our server brought our food, I said something to him. He brought her to our table, and I told her what I saw and that she should NEVER play with her hair by the food. I told her that if she needs to redo her ponytail, she needs to do it in the bathroom and wash her hands afterward. I wasn't nasty or anything, I just told her like it was, and wanted her to know that people can and do see her. Her hair might be very clean, but I don't want to eat it! The next time we were there, she came up to me and thanked me for pointing out what she had done. She apologized and said she is more aware of what she was doing.

NEVER NEVER NEVER let your customers see you smoking! This is a nasty habit!! I have it and I don't care if my server smokes; however, they better wash their hands when finished. If you have a smoke on your break, please do it in a spot where the clientele can't see you. Some people are against smoking big time and may think you are working to support your smoking habit. They may also think that if you smoke, you do other things as well, and this could be reflected in your tip.

Wait staff, you are **NOT** supposed to be human! You can't be in a bad mood. You can't have a bad day and the most important thing is – you can't sneeze!!! The normal reaction when one sneezes is to cover your mouth with your hand. **NO, NO, NO,** do **NOT** use your hand!

If you must sneeze when at a table taking an order, sneeze into your shoulder. Turning your head so your mouth is in your shoulder and then sneeze. Should you be carrying food or drinks do everything you can to not sneeze in the food or drinks.

I was carrying two plates once and had to sneeze. I held the plates up over my head and went down on one knee and sneezed into the floor. It was *NOT* pretty, but it was effective.

Being a server is *VERY* hard and exhausting work. You are on your feet sometimes eight hours at a time continuously moving and eating your food so fast that you don't even taste it. It's also a very rewarding job. There is so much money to be made and you are so lucky that you get to meet new people all the time. The amount of money you make is entirely up to you and the job is what you make it. **YOU** are the one choosing to have a great shift or a lousy one. Choose greatness!

Chapter

III

Kitchen

Staff

"Consistency equals repeat customers"

The cooks are the backbone of the establishment! The cooks **MUST** be consistent in the way **YOU**, the owner, wants the food to look and taste. Consistency equals repeat customers. There are many cooks that feel <u>their</u> way is so much better than the boss' way. It's imperative that all the cooks be on the same page, so the food always comes out the same. The same *MUST* always be the owner's way! Not a new cook's "better" way. It's the owner's restaurant not the cook's and if the cook's way was so excellent, the cook would have his/her own restaurant. A cook can always make suggestions to the owner. Perhaps they will let the cook try something different, but if they say no, leave it alone.

If you have an imaginative cook, let them experiment a little, but not with your regular menu items. These items must be consistent, as these are the items that will be served by every cook you hire. Let your cook create something and make it a special and see how it goes. It can't hurt anything. It may increase business and it may go over so well that it becomes a weekly or monthly special. There is nothing wrong with a little inventing, just be careful the cook doesn't break the bank with the items they intend to use. You don't want them to create a dish that costs you $29.99 to make and you must charge $39.95 to make your money back!

Cooks should always wear a hat or hair net. I know hair nets look dumb, but like I said about the server, I don't want to eat your hair. Oh, and cooks must **ALWAYS ALWAYS ALWAYS** wear a shirt with sleeves. I know how hot is in the kitchen, but there is nothing grosser than a cook coming out front for a cold drink and raising his arm to reach for a cup and you see his sweaty, hairy armpits! UGH!! What would you do? I think I would throw up! That is just disgusting!

Dishwashers, I know you have the worst job of all, but please take pride in it. You are the least paid, the hardest working, and you receive the least recognition for a job well done. Face it, your job is **NASTY**!!!! Scraping plates, washing lipstick of cups, scrubbing caked on food off silverware, etc., is degrading. I also know that the only time someone speaks to you (usually) is to bitch about a dirty fork, plate or glass. But, please know that we really **DO APPRECIATE YOU**! We just don't show it often enough. So, what happens when the dishwasher calls in sick? **PANIC MODE**!!! "What? You want ME to wash dishes?" Everyone freaks out and acts like they are so much better than the dishwasher. What a joke. No one is better than anyone else in the restaurant business. Everyone must work together to make the restaurant work!!

When the food is good, the cook gets the recognition. When the service is good, the wait staff gets the recognition. But what happens when the dishes come out sparkling clean? People just say, "That's their job." You know I'm right. Half the time we don't even know the dishwasher's name. We're all guilty of this. You never think to thank the dishwasher or praise their work. It's almost like the cooks and wait staff are the children and must be praised to continue to do a good job. Not the dishwasher, they keep washing those dishes no matter what.

Suppose every restaurant had their cooks and wait staff wash dishes for one shift. What do you think they would take away from that experience? Example: the cook makes a very large pot of mashed potatoes and believe me, as a dishwasher, you will wash many, many, many very large pots. He or she lets the potatoes sit in the pot for a long time before transferring them into a container. He then takes the very large pot over to the dishwasher and the potatoes are welded stuck to the inside of the pot. Now, you must soak and scrub that pot to no end to get the potatoes off.

Not only are you now infuriated at the cook, you will resent that cook and probably not want to work with them again. Imagine if the cook washed dishes for one shift and that happened to him. Do you think he would do things the same way again? Hopefully not, but you never know. Some people are just plain mean and nasty!

Everyone should know about the other's job. Each role is hard and stressful in its own way, and besides, what's wrong with all the employees knowing what the others go through?

Chapter

IV

Bartenders

"ALWAYS pay attention to YOUR bar!"

Oh, you busy little bartenders! You have the best job in a restaurant. You can change a person's entire disposition! You have the power!!! The most important thing for you to remember is…<u>ALWAYS</u> pay attention to **YOUR** bar!! I don't care how many bartenders are working. Each one of you needs to act as if you are the only one on duty.

Trust me, you can carry a conversation with a customer and pay attention to the other customers at the same time! IMAGINE THAT! It's called "**MULTI-TASKING**" and if you don't know how to do it, you don't need to be a bartender. You are the ONE employee that will be conversing with one or more customers while waiting on other customers and employees at the same time! You are the one the customer comes to in order to solve their problems in life. They expect you to listen to them and with any luck have answers for whatever they are going through.

As a bartender, you also need to be aware of EVERYTHING around you. If you see that a server is busy and they had ordered drinks, instead of letting the drinks sit there until the server can get back to them, DELIVER THE DRINKS YOURSELF! You will **NOT** hurt yourself! **I PROMISE**! It will make the business look better and showcase you as a more valuable employee and team worker.

Remember, you never know who the customer could be. You may find yourself out of work one day and go to another restaurant or lounge to apply for a job. The owner where you're applying could be the owner you delivered drinks to or went out of your way to serve. He may have thought you were a very good employee and team player hiring you on the spot. Of course, the opposite could be true as well. Especially if the customers can see you doing nothing while their drinks sit on the bar getting warm or watered down. He may NOT hire you for that reason alone.

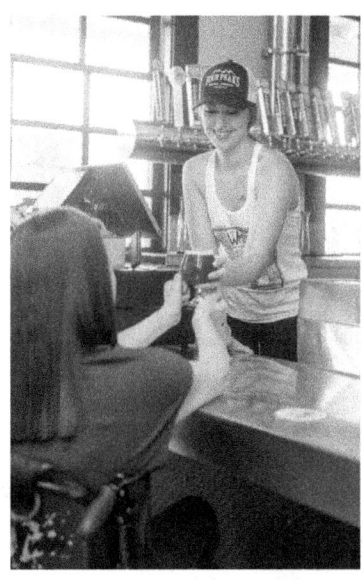

Other business owners will notice how you do your job. Example: a guy is sitting at your bar and you're not busy, but the servers are. You make some drinks and set them in the service station for pick up. Since you're not busy, you go back to watching the show on the television while the drinks are sitting there and the ice is melting, or the beer is getting warm. Maybe you're not watching TV. Perhaps you're filing your nails, eating dinner, or the <u>ABSOLUTE WORST OF ALL,</u> talking on your phone!!!! Whatever you are doing, this guy sees you doing NOTHING and the customers drinks going flat.

The server finally arrives and delivers the drinks. Now he/she must bring the draft beer back because it is warm and flat. Who suffers from this? You? The server? Maybe the server, but mostly the establishment all due to the bartender's lack of initiative! Now, back to the guy watching all this happening. All that time he is wondering to himself, *now why didn't he/she deliver those drinks when there was nothing else to do? The ticket has the table number on it.* This is even more important if you get a percentage of the server's tips at the end of the night. Remember, happy customers equal more money for everyone!

Let me reiterate again.

EVERYONE HAS TO WORK TOGETHER TO MAKE IT WORK!!!!

Chapter V

Employers

"Let your employees know they are excellent at what they do and that you appreciate their hard work, and they will continue to excel at their job!"

¡	You are the only one that needs to know how everything associated with how your business runs. It is good for other employees to know what the other jobs entail. You never know when you may need someone to fill in, even if only for an hour. You don't need everyone knowing everything about all the jobs, just enough to get by in case of emergency. It can NEVER hurt for servers to know what cooks go through and vice versa.

¡	Make the schedules to reflect an employee's shift beginning ten or fifteen minutes early. This SHOULD ensure the employee arrive on time. You are an employer, not a babysitter. I know too many people that think if their job starts at seven o'clock, this means they leave their house at seven o'clock. TRUTH!!!

¡   As a business owner, you have an extremely difficult job! You must be strict with employees, but you don't want to be too strict where they won't respect you or your business. You can discipline an employee however you see fit, but please, **NEVER, NEVER, NEVER discipline or criticize an employee in front of others.** There is no quicker way to lose your reputation and value from the employee and whoever saw and heard you. This is also a very good way to get ripped off by that employee.

¡   If you have a wonderful greeter, make sure they know you appreciate them! It is awfully important to keep that greeter cheerful to ensure they want to come to work. Make them feel they are an intricate part of the organization. If your greeter comes to work dressed sloppy, send them home! They are the first person your customers will see, and first impressions are everything!!!

¡ Make sure your wait staff knows they are first-rate and that you appreciate their hard work. If you cannot do this sincerely, get new wait staff. There are many people willing to work and do a good job. Sometimes it just takes a while to find them. Be patient as you may have to go through some REAL terrible servers before the exceptional ones. If your server comes to work looking disheveled, please send them home!

¡ If your cook comes to work wearing a sleeveless shirt, looks dirty or smells badly, please send them home! Let your cook(s) know what an awesome job they did, even more so if it was an exceptionally busy night.

¡ Make sure your dishwashers feel like they are part of the team! This is one of the most forgotten employees! Let them know you couldn't do it without them!

¡ You are as much at fault if your business fails as the employees. Your employees are only as good as their leader.

REMEMBER!!!! Let your employees know they are valued and that you appreciate them and the hard work they do for your business. A little gratitude goes a long way!!

Everyone must work together to make it work!!!